Preface

The second biggest success in my career was being fired by Mike Milken, the Junk Bond King.

I was Vice President and Treasurer of Safeguard Business Systems in 1989, when we started hearing rumblings about a takeover by Mike Milken and Drexel Burnham. Mike Milken was already in trouble with securities police, charged with 98 felony counts for fraud, racketeering and insider trading. In 1988, Mike's friends and colleagues began wearing T-shirts proclaiming, "Mike Milken, We Believe In You."

On March 31, 1989, an advertisement ran in the New York Times, the Wall Street Journal, the Washington Post, and the Los Angeles Times, which proclaimed:

"Mike cares about people. Mike has always performed according to the highest standards of professionalism, honesty, integrity and ethical conduct. We know Mike Milken, and based on our firsthand experience with him, we believe in him."

Shortly after the advertisement appeared, in marched a phalanx of

Wharton MBAs, who began digging through Safeguard's files. I guess I was my usual snarky self because I was deemed uncooperative by the Wharton MBAs. The Wharton MBAs were one trick ponies - they learned Mike Milken's theory, which turned out to be flawed, as I explain later in this paper. Damned if I was going to do their job for them when I knew I was about to be fired. Milken modus operandi: he fired all the treasurers.

Soon, Vincent G. "Buck" Bell called me into his office and told me in his fatherly way to cooperate with the Wharton MBAs. A lightbulb went off in my head—I suddenly realized that I was the only person at Safeguard Business Systems who understood what I did.

Basically, I set up SBS Leasing Company to buy deals that used Safeguard's tax appetite to mainline earnings per share. Totally legal at the time, thanks to our sometimes ill-informed Federal governance system.

The year just finished was the last year I could use that trick and I didn't have another one up my sleeve. My leasing partners were moving on, all I could do was hope that none of our deals went bad or Safeguard and I would be in deep shit.

I also knew that if I told the Wharton MBAs everything they would walk away from the deal. So I said to Buck, "I will answer all their questions honestly and forthrightly."

And I did.

The Wharton MBAs had no idea how to ask the questions, the deal went through. Buck and all Safeguard's corporate officers except me, got golden parachutes. Buck patiently explained to me why I didn't deserve a golden parachute. A Safeguard board member slipped me his attorney's card and told me sue for a settlement. He told me I would be blacklisted in the corporate community, which is why I switched to the non-profit world, primarily community and educational foundations. Stories for another time.

I took some solace in the fact that all Safeguard employees received small payouts into an IRA (individual retirement plan) and most kept their jobs, at least until the efficiency experts arrived.

Why this preface to my paper? I still had not resolved the unfairness of it all when I enrolled in the Dynamics of Organization Program at the University of Pennsylvania several years later. Foulie Perlmutter was the wife of

Howard Perlmutter, Dean of the Wharton School of Business, at the time. Foulie was a kindly, caring and demanding professor, who always challenged her students to do their best work. This paper was part of my healing process.

What is the biggest success in my career, you ask, if being fired by Mike Milken is the second biggest?

I was the only old white woman speaker at the Inaugural Black Tech Week in Miami Florida (2015). I am grateful to Felecia Hatcher and Derick Pearson for the opportunity. I was on a panel with five young black men; the host was a twenty-two year old venture capitalist from Detroit. I have followed the career of these young men and they continue to excel in their careers.

The young men answered all some very tough questions from the audience. A young woman from the audience asked me a detailed finance question with lots of numbers. I answered, "My work is to create community, the place these young men and their families live with all the services they need for a happy life, the bodegas, the bike shops, the restaurants, bars and taco stands, local schools, etc."

Felecia and Derick apologized to me after the session. I said, "For what? I got exactly what I wanted. A few folks, mostly older, came up to me and told me how wonderful my concept was! The community needs young men with passion and enthusiasm to make money and, as they get older, they will learn the importance of community."

Felecia, Derick and the entire Black Tech Week Team have continued to soar to new heights. Mike Milken went to jail and Drexel Burnham went bankrupt.

Table of Contents

"HE WHO HAS THE GOLD

MAKES THE RULES"[1]

Introduction

In the <u>Study of History</u>, Arnold Toynbee documented the rise and fall of twenty—one great civilizations. Their demise came not from natural disasters or invasion, but from failures in internal governance. The institutions and practices that were responsible for success of the civilization were taken to extremes and ultimately caused the decline.[2]

Industrial society (Paradigm I) has reached a point when a paradigm change must take place to insure survival. Our society is in the first stage of a second order change, the stage of decline. There are many warning signals.[3] We need to understand and heed these signals so we are free to move forward.

Today, there is evidence of dysfunction in all major institutions of Paradigm I. This paper will analyze the United States industrial enterprise — the corporation. It will give examples of successful strategies which have become destructive by continual adaptation. Finally it will give reason to hope that industrial society can transition to Paradigm S, a symbiotic partnership that "seeks a new set of balances between autonomy and interdependence, cooperation (win—win) and competition."[4]

The United States Corporation

In Paradigm I, "the private corporation is designed to pursue its own ends— competition with other corporations. The principle of competitive individualism has provided the basis for the growth dynamic of industrial societies."[5]

This competitive individualism that fueled growth in the past has become a liability because the other societal institutions have begun to change, i.e. the Icarus Paradox applied to the corporation of Paradigm I. The

"Captains of Industry" have recognized that a shift has begun to take place. Their solution to dealing with the change is to do more of what has worked in the past and do it more vigorously.[6]

This has created a "feeding frenzy." A strategy is designed and implemented in one situation and it works. It is then adapted and implemented over and over again, becoming progressively more destructive.

Our system of capital markets evolved because society needed a mechanism to fund the huge investments required by our factories and other industries.

Capitalism was built on the premise that superior rewards would accrue to those individuals who were willing to risk their capital. Capitalism did not promise "fairness" or "equality" to all members of society. However, it did promise that greater risks were required to enjoy greater rewards.

As the industrial revolution progressed, the capitalists that emerged continually sought to minimize their risks and maximize rewards. Society sought to maintain the equilibrium between risk and reward. As a result of this process to maintain the equilibrium, labor unions were born and government regulations were drafted and became law. By continually refining this process, the quality of life for society improved and the rewards that accrued to the capitalists became greater.

In recent years, the equilibrium has been disturbed in increasingly destructive ways—warning signals that radical change is needed. Some examples of these warning signals follow.

Junk Bonds. Mike Milken of Drexel Burnham developed a market in low and unrated, high-yield bonds. He based his thesis on "junk" bonds on a study by W. Braddock Hickman.

Hickman demonstrated that from 1900 to 1943, a diversified long-term portfolio of low-grade bonds yielded a higher rate of return, without any greater risk, than a comparable portfolio of blue-chip, top-rated bonds. A study from 1945 to 1965 reached the same conclusion.[7]

Milken's original thesis was based in fact; however, he continually refined the "junk" bond concept without assessing the impact of these changes on his original thesis.

- Drexel pioneered the issuance of "junk" bonds that were sold in the publicly traded securities markets. The bonds in Hickman's study were originally issued by investment grade companies which were downgraded or they were issued privately.

- Drexel created the public market for "junk" bonds. Before Milken, "junk" bonds were not liquid and traded privately.

- Milken controlled the market for "junk" bonds through his extensive network of issuers and investors. In fact, he controlled both buyers and sellers. He was indicted for securities fraud as a result of some of these connections.

Milken became obsessed with keeping absolute control of the "junk" bond market and generating ever higher fees and spreads on trades. Control was the game and money was the scorecard.

In December 1986, Drexel financed the takeover of Safeguard Business Systems by Mason—Best, a newly formed merchant bank. Safeguard's revenues for 1986, its best year ever, were approximately $250 million, or 45% of Milken's compensation from Drexel for 1987. The price that Mason-Best paid based on analysis provided by Drexel could not be supported by the cash flow of the company. The company went through a series of financial restructurings which ultimately resulted in a bankruptcy and a "downsizing" to approximately 50% of its former size, with virtually a 100% staff turnover.

In 1990, Lipper Analytical Services reported a ten year average yield on "junk" bonds of 145%, as compared to 207% for stocks and 177% for Treasuries, showing clearly that the average investor did not receive superior returns on "junk" bonds. However, Milken and his inner circle extracted huge profits. Some profits were made legally through "spreads" on trades (the market was unregulated; hence, Drexel set the spread) and high investment banking fees. Some profits were made illegally by trading insider information among a select group. In the end, "it was the criminals who earned astronomical yields."[8]

Savings and Loans. The savings and loan industry grew up after the Great Depression to finance the purchases of homes by American families. The types of investments that they made, the interest that paid on deposits, and the interest charged on mortgages were all tightly regulated. In return for low interest rates, deposits were insured up to $40,000 per depositor by the Federal Savings & Loan Insurance Corporation (FSLIC).

In 1980, Congress passed a billing removing interest rate controls and increasing FSLIC insurance to $100,000 per depositor. In 1982, President Reagan signed the Garn—St. Germain Act removing other restrictive Federal regulations and deregulating the industry. This developed "a pervasive feeling that anything not actually illegal or specifically prohibited by thrift regulators was fair game."[9]

S&Ls began investing in "junk bonds"

and speculative real estate deals. The industry attracted a large criminal element in addition to enterprising entrepreneurs driven by greed and glory. The industry went from being a highly regulated, prudent business bordering on a community service to an unregulated "Casino." This was all financed by the tax payers of America through the FSLIC deposit insurance.

"Deregulation as it was carried out during the Reagan administration benefitted not mainstream business . . . but financial rainmakers like Mike Milken . . . and a host of others who created nothing of lasting value while siphoning off billions of dollars from our national treasury."[10] The "bailout" of the Savings & Loan industry is estimated to cost the American taxpayer more than $500 billion.

Executive Compensation. Industrial society has always espoused a hierarchal corporate compensation plan. The owners of the company received greater rewards because their capital was at risk. Through their unions, workers demanded fair and just wages; however, they did not challenge the owners right to greater compensation.

Top executives today are employees in the same sense that other workers are employees. Their "ownership" of the company is limited to stock ownership. Usually, this stock ownership represents a small percentage of ownership in the corporation, although it may represent a significant portion of the executive's net worth. Often this stock is accumulated through stock option plans or "sign on" bonuses rather than investment of capital.

Executive pay became a political issue on President George H.W. Bush's trip to Japan when it was revealed that Lee Iacocca's salary was $4.5 million in 1990, while Shoichiro Toyoda of Toyota earned $690, 000. Iacocca of Chrysler, one of the financially weakest auto makers, was in Japan to complain about unfair competition from the Japanese auto makers. Perhaps a reevaluation of the executive compensation structure would make the American automobile industry more competitive.[11]

In 1981, the compensation of the 25 highest paid US Executives ranged from a low of $1.5 million to a high of $5.7 million. In 1988, the range was from a low of $5.9 million to a high of $40.1 million.[12] In seven years, the compensation of CEOs increased 397%.

This happened at a time when

companies were downsizing and cutting wages and benefits for other workers. The divergence between the pay of hourly—paid production workers and CEO also increase during the 1980s. In 1968, the average CEO earned 25 times the average annual pay of an hourly—paid production worker. This difference increased to 29 times by 1978 and to 36 times by 1988.[13]

While the earnings of the top executives of industrialist firms seem out of line with their contribution, they are paltry in comparison to the compensation that Wall Street investment bankers awarded themselves.

In 1986, the bonus pool for the "junk" bond department of Drexel Burnham was $700 million. Mike Milken awarded $550 million of this pool to himself. Jim Dahl, the top bond salesman in the department was awarded $10 million. Dahl said he felt he was entitled to more. Mike's reply: "Jim, I really can't pay you more than me. Now that wouldn't be fair, would it?"[14] Mike didn't think that $550 million was enough. He was angry about the size of the bonus pool.

Merger Mania. Companies have routinely been bought and sold in industrialized society. The M&A process gave privately held and family owned businesses the opportunity to cash out. It gave corporations the opportunity to buy synergistic product lines and achieve economies of scale.

The 1960s saw the rise of the conglomerators such as Harold Geneen of ITT and Charlie Bluhdorn of Gulf and Western. They were aggressive entrepreneurs who believed that good management was not industry specific, hence their managers and control systems could be effectively used in any industry or environment. The conglomerators were arrogant and reckless in their approach, but they did not acquire companies which did not want to be acquired.[15]

This changed in the 1980s as a new breed emerged—the corporate raiders who acquired companies in hostile takeovers, using O.P.M. (Other People's Money). Ross Perot, founder of Electronic Data Systems, describes them, "To say these guys are entrepreneurs is like saying that Jesse James was an entrepreneur. In my day, you could make lots of money creating a new product or backing a new company. But now, if you're an investment banker, you can make many times that amount of money in three or four weeks—and through the miracle of junk bonds leave all the risk with the pension funds, S&Ls and banks, all of which are insured by the government. . . Now it's the taxpayer, the average citizen, who's become the entrepreneur, in fact, with all the risk and very little of the reward."[16]

Peter Drucker states, "The fear of the raider is undoubtedly the largest single cause for the increasing tendency of American companies to manage for the short term and let the future go hang. . . the record is poor for all companies that have been merged. . . Only three out of ten such acquiring companies do as well two years later as they did before the merger. But the record of companies that have been acquired in a hostile takeover is uniformly dismal."[17]

In the case of Simplicity Pattern, a series of four "raiders" bought and sold the Company from 1982 to 1990. In the process, they personally made tens of millions of dollars. The company, its employees and the American taxpayer did not fare as well. The raiders:

- Drained $100 million from bank and investment accounts.

- Drained $10.7 million from the pension fund.

- Jobs were eliminated, wages and benefits were reduced.

- Corporate taxes on $200 million were eliminated.

- "Junk bonds" issued by Drexel Burnham financed two "raiders."

Company defaulted on "junk bonds" and bank loans.[18]

This scenario was repeated many times during the 1980s. The raiders "won" and the rest of the country "lost"—the ultimate win-lose situation. O.P.M. was our money—yours and mine, not just an acronym for a financing technique taught at business schools.

Downsizing. Downsizing became a buzz word for the eighties. The reasons for downsizing were many including deregulation, increased competition—foreign and domestic, technological changes, and the merger and acquisition frenzy.

Union workers have been used to layoffs, often balanced by periods of high overtime, as companies adjust to the ebb and flow of orders for industrial products. However, with "white collar" workers, companies preached the doctrine of paternalism, promising employees, either implicitly or explicitly, a job for life. This paternalism was not a gesture of generosity, but a reaction to the union movement. If they treated the white collar workers as well or better than the union workers, these employees would have no reason to seek out a union.

This worked for both parties until the recession of 1981—1982, when US corporations recognized that the bulge in the corporate bureaucracy was interfering with their competitiveness in the world markets.[19] There were no laws guaranteeing employees a job for life, and there were few white collar unions to negotiate with, so corporations broke the lifetime employment contract. They "substituted not a new contract, but a sort of threat. It was: We can fire you at any time, for any reason."[20]

When companies downsize, "first they get rid of people, then they make some decision about organizing those who remain. Only eventually, as they find their lean staff cannot do all the work that remains, do these businesses start to consider work priorities."[21]

This process strips people of their self-respect and dignity and causes a deep sense of alienation. Among those that remain, there is a diminished sense of loyalty and enthusiasm for their work. Although staffs are cut, the functions do not go away and the "survivors" are often asked to perform the job of two people. "A study of auto—related companies in the Midwest found that nearly half of the two thousand managers polled were working harder than two years earlier."[22] Burnout from overwork is becoming a problem for companies and has been dubbed the disease of the nineties.

Paradoxes

In these five examples of dysfunctional adaptation, it is interesting to note that women were either underrepresented or did not participate in all but one area.

- **Junk Bonds.** In <u>Den of Thieves</u>, which chronicled the insider trading scandal, only two women were indicted, Lisa Ann Jones and Pamela Monzert. Lisa Ann Jones was a trading assistant who did not profit from insider trading, but remained loyal to Mike Milken and in the process perjured herself. Pamela Monzert is identified on page 394 as "another high yield bond employee," with no mention of her involvement.

- **Savings and Loans.** In <u>Inside Job</u>, Beverly Haines of the Centennial Savings was the only female Savings and Loan executive convicted. Her crime was limited to embezzlement at Centennial Savings; she was not plugged into the nationwide network which systematically looted the Savings and Loans.

- **Merger Mania.** The guest list for the 1986 Drexel High—Yield Bond Conference, nicknamed the Predator's Ball, lists 50 "self-made millionaires," most of whom are also corporate raiders. None of the 50 were women.[23]

- **Executive Compensation.** There are no women on the list of the 25 highest paid US Executives for either 1988 or 1981.

- **Downsizing.** "Women were far more likely to than men to lose their jobs or get their wages cut than men."[24] Generally, women had less seniority than men and they were more apt to hold staff positions. Women were "downsized" more often than men.

Conclusion

Industrial society is a patriarchal society. Competitive individuals are men who manage by authority. Women are tolerated in factories and in other roles in corporations, only when it makes economic sense and increases profits.

During World War II, women staffed most factories because most able bodied young men were off at war. Without women, the factories would not have been able to produce the goods required to support the war effort. Many factories would have sat idle and "Captains of Industry" would have incurred huge losses.

Given this bleak alternative, corporations were able to solve issues which haunt us today. For example, during World War II, Federally funded day care centers were set up for the children of women who worked in industries which were vital to the nation's defense. These day care centers, which provided excellent care, allowed women to enter the work force in large numbers. At the end of the war, the men returned, the women were fired and the day care centers were disbanded.

During the last twenty five years, women have returned to the work force in large numbers. They have returned because the supply of male workers has not been adequate to fill all the jobs in the work place, not because of an increase in awareness of the rights of women or because of affirmative action. However, we have still not been able to solve the problem of quality day care, a problem which was solved overnight during World War II.

The 1980s were the decade of greed. The Wall Street investment banks have always controlled large blocks of securities and cash, financed huge deals and paid big salaries. In the eighties, none of the past successes were good enough or big enough as Wall Street embarked on a "feeding frenzy" to create ever bigger deals and to make more and more money. Money became an end unto itself, i.e. "He who has the Gold makes the rules."[25]

Competitive individualism which is the foundation for the Paradigm I corporation is in its death throes. It will not die easily because the "Captains" will not fit in a Paradigm S corporate society. Competitive individualism is a male model and virtually all "Captains" are men.

Women did not participate in this "feeding frenzy." Some would attribute this to "The Glass Ceiling," the transparent barrier that keeps women from rising above a certain level in the corporate world. They would demand equal rights for women to behave as destructively and outrageously as some of the "Captains" of industry have behaved. Another answer may be that women's strengths are not the same as men's and these differences mitigated against their involvement in the "feeding frenzy."

The traits exhibited by the "Captains" included rugged individualism, aggressive competitiveness, a need for absolute control, and a win—lose orientation. Women are more comfortable cooperating, in a win—win situation.

A symbiotic societal model(paradigm S) embraces traits such as cooperation, teaching, facilitating, and nurturing which are generally labeled as feminine traits or at least androgynous. Howard Perlmutter states that paradigm S will become more widely accepted as opportunities for "having successful experiences building symbiotic partnerships, enterprises, communities, and other groups which are mutually beneficial, based on openness, trust, and mutual respect.

"The symbiotic partnership experience involves the finding of shared objectives, among dissimilar institutions, in which the partners, as equals, build on their own strengths and reduce each other's limitations, pooling capabilities to take on tasks which none of the partners could undertake alone."[26]

Women are comfortable with the concept of symbiosis because they bear children. Much of the struggle in child rearing is helping the child to develop from a total symbiotic state to an independent ego state while still retaining the nurture and caring which will sustain her/him throughout life.

Most individuals do not totally succeed in this struggle, with up to 97% experiencing some dysfunction in their lives. In 1945, Elton Mayo attributed this to the social disruption of industrial society. He saw a large increase in the number of unhappy individuals. "Step by step with our economic progress there has been a destruction of individual significance in living for the majority of citizens."[27] Today our collective sense of disenfranchisement has increased as we endure change at a frenetic pace.

There is much evidence that American business is in the midst of crisis that requires a paradigm shift. A paradigm shift is painful and requires that the population give up long held ideas which no longer work. "These are exhausted ideas, like dead stars, in the American political atmosphere, which nonetheless remain central to the way certain subjects are discussed and to the formulation of national policy."[28] Our current response has been to refine these old ideas until they become destructive and hasten our decline as an economic power.

Instead we should examine alternatives to Paradigm I and become open to new structures which will lead to a "kinder, gentler America," as advocated by President George H.W. Bush.[29]

Since 1980, US business has discovered the work of W. Edwards Deming. Deming is an American statistician who taught the Japanese the modern management techniques that revitalized Japanese industry after World War II. Deming believes that employees take pride in their work. When they are given the support of management, they will improve the quality of the work that they produce. This will make the corporation competitive in the market place, will allow the firm to stay in business, and will create more jobs. Deming uses cross functional teams to accomplish his objectives.

Deming states, "Paper entrepreneurism. . . .does not create wealth. It does not make the pie bigger. There's a road map to follow to make the pie bigger. Did you ever stop to think of the power of teamwork? We don't have it in this country. It is every man for himself. Call it rugged individualism . . . and the American style of management creates it — there cannot be teamwork. . ."[30]

The Deming management method

offers hope a paradigm shift is beginning. It is based on teamwork rather than competitive individualism. It believes that workers are interested in doing a good job and thus provides with the satisfaction of a job well done.

To paraphrase the biologist Lewis Thomas, survival of the fittest doesn't mean that nature is red in tooth and claw, as the 19th century read the message of evolution, or that only the strongest, most dominating, and the shrewdest will win. The fittest who survive are those who cooperate best with other living things.[31]

The new Golden Rule for the 21st century and the plague for the walls in our offices will read:

The survivors are those who cooperate best with other living things.

Appendix

Business Leaders Take Ad That Backs Milken [FULL TRANSCRIPT]

By Douglas C. McGill, *New York Times*, April 1, 1989

A message first seen last year on T-shirts worn by friends and colleagues of 50Michael Milken appeared yesterday as the headline of a full-page advertisement signed by dozens of prominent business executives: "Mike Milken, We Believe in You."

The advertisement's two-paragraph statement praised Mr. Milken, the former executive of Drexel Burnham Lambert Inc. who pioneered the widespread use of "junk bonds." Signers of the advertisement include prominent lawyers, financial executives and the chief executives of dozens of companies, like Mattel Inc., Kindercare Inc., Chock Full o' Nuts and the

Western Union Corporation.

The ad appeared two days after Mr.
Milken was indicted by a Federal grand
jury on various securities law
violations. The Government, which had
sought Tuesday's indictment for
almost three years, has charged him
with 98 felony counts of fraud,
racketeering and insider trading, and it
is seeking unprecedented penalties of
$1.8 billion against him and two other
defendants.

The advertisement is the strongest,
most public support yet offered to Mr.
Milken by members of the business
community, many of whom have been

personally enriched by his financial
dealings, and who say that the entire
American business world has been
greatly strengthened by his
achievements.

> **'We Believe in Him'**
>
> "Mike cares about people," read
> the advertisement, which ran
> yesterday in The New York
> Times, The Wall Street Journal,
> The Washington Post and The
> Los Angeles Times. "Mike has
> always performed according to
> the highest standards of
> professionalism, honesty,
> integrity and ethical conduct. We
> know Mike Milken, and based on
> our firsthand experience with
> him, we believe in him."

In interviews yesterday, many of the
executives who signed the ad said

they had done so not only out of personal loyalty to Mr. Milken, but because they believed the Government's handling of the case had raised serious questions of civil liberties, business principles and other issues.

"It's been a McCarthy-like witch hunt," said Ralph Ingersoll 2d, the chairman of the Ingersoll Publications Company, a newspaper publishing concern in Princeton, N.J. "The whole thrust of this campaign has been to deprive Milken of his civil rights, and force on the public the assumption that he's guilty."

Leaks to the Press Seen

Mr. Ingersoll contended that for more than two years, the Government agencies pursuing Mr. Milken - the Securities and Exchange Commission and the United States Attorney's office for the Southern District of New York - have leaked to the press information that has damaged Mr. Milken's reputation, and his chance for a fair trial.

Over the last six years, Mr. Ingersoll said, Drexel Burnham Lambert has been investment banker to his firm, as it has issued high-yield bonds to replace bank debts that it owed.

The advertisements supporting Mr. Milken cost around $200,000 altogether and were paid for with contributions from the signers. They were organized by Selig Zises, the chairman of Integrated Resources, an investment firm.

"I kept reading about somebody I didn't know in the newspapers," Mr. Zises said yesterday. "From our personal experience, we know someone who has integrity and sensitivity, and we certainly believe that until it's proven otherwise, he's innocent."

Rudolph W. Giuliani, the former United

States Attorney who initiated the Government's case against Mr. Milken, declined to answer specific charges, but he maintained that "the conduct of my office has been entirely ethical and proper," and that "this case will get an answer in court."

John Sturc, the associate director of the division of enforcement for the S.E.C., denied yesterday that his agency had been the source of leaks to the press. Comparing the intricacies of the preparation involved in the Milken case to the Watergate and Iran-contra cases, he added, "Complex matters take a significant amount of time, and there's nothing new in that."

Footnotes

[1] A modern day version of the Golden Rule as expressed by J. Pfeffer, Power in Organizations, Pitman, 1981, p. 101. A plaque expressing the same thought hung in Martin Seigel's office, "Whoever has the most at the end, wins." Martin Seigel was an investment banker with Kidder Peabody who plead guilty to conspiracy to violate the securities laws and tax evasion as part of the Milken/Boesky insider trading investigations.

[2] Miller, The Icarus Paradox, Harvard Business Press, 1990, p. 265.

[3] Levy, "Second—Order Planned Change: Definition and Conceptualization", Organizational Dynamics, Summer 1986.

[4] Perlmutter, "Building the Symbiotic Societal Enterprise: A Social Architecture for the Future," World Futures, Volume 19, p. 281.

[5] Perlmutter & Trist, "Paradigms for Societal Transition. " Human Relations, 39(1) 1986.

[6] Miller, p. 3 .

[7] Stewart, Den of Thieves, Simon & Schuster, 1991, p. 45.

[8] Stewart, P. 430.

[9] Pizzo, Fricker, & Muolo, Inside Job - The Looting of America's Savings & Loans, McGraw—Hill Publishing Co. 1989, p. 495.

[10] Pizzo, Fricker & Muolo, P. 494.

[11] Caprino, The Philadelphia Inquirer, November 1991.

[12] Phillips, The Politics of the Rich and Poor, Random House, 1990. p. 179.

[13] Phillips, p. 181.

[14] Stewart, p. 207-208.

[15] Miller, pp. 51-93.

[16] Phillips, p. 72.

[17] Drucker, The Frontiers of Management, E.P.Dutton, 1986.

[18] Barrett and Steele, "Part 7: Simplicity Pattern Irresistible to Raiders," The Philadelphia Inquirer, October 26, 1991.

[19] Tomasko, Downsizing: Reshaping the Corporation for the Future, Amacom, 1987.

[20] Bennett, The Death of the Organization Man, Simon & Schuster, 1990.

[21] Tomasko, p. 190.

[22] Schor, The Overworked American, Basic Books, 1991.

[23] Stewart, p. 222.

[24] Faludi, Backlash: The Undeclared War Against American Women, Crown Publishers, Inc., 1991, p. 368.

[25] Pfeffer, p. 101.

[26] Perlmutter, p. 283.

[27] Mayo, <u>The Social Problems of an Industrial Civilization</u>, Harvard Business School, 1945, pp. 5-15.

[28] Pfaff, <u>Barbarian Sentiments: How the American Century Ends</u>, Hill & Wang, 1990.

[29] Phillips, p. 152.

[30] Walton, <u>The Deming Management Method</u>, Perigee Books, 1986.

[31] Perlmutter, p. 284.

Bibliography

Bennett, Amanda. The Death of the Organization Man. Simon & Schuster, 1990.

Barrett, Donald L. and Steele, James M. "Part 7: Simplicity Pattern Irresistible to Raiders," The Philadelphia Inquirer, October 26, 1991.

Caprino, Maryann. The Philadelphia Inquirer, November 1991.

Drucker, Peter F. The Frontiers of Management. E.P.Dutton, 1986.

Faludi, Susan. Backlash: The Undeclared War Against American Women. Crown Publishers, Inc., 1991.

Levy, Amir. "Second-Order Planned Change: Definition and Conceptualization," Organizational Dynamics, Summer 1986.

Mayo, Elton. The Social Problems of an Industrial Civilization. Harvard Business School, 1945, pp. 5-15.

Miller, Danny. The Icarus Paradox. Harvard Business Press, 1990.

Morrison, Ann M. , White, Randall P. and van Velsor, Ellen. Breaking the Glass Ceiling. Addison—Wesley Publishing, Inc., 1987.

Naisbitt, John and Aburdene, Patricia. Re-inventing the Corporation. Warner Books, 1985.

Perlmutter, Howard V. "Building the Symbiotic Societal Enterprise: A Social Architecture for the Future," World Futures, Volume 19, pp. 271-284.

Perlmutter, Howard and Trist, Eric. "Paradigms for Societal Transition," Human Relations, 39(1) 1986.

Pfaff, W. Barbarian Sentiments: How the American Century Ends. Hill & Wang, 1990.

Pfeffer, J. Power in Organizations. Pitman, 1981.

Phillips, Kevin. The Politics of the Rich and Poor. Random House, 1990.

Pizzo, Stephen, Fricker, Mary & Muolo, Paul. Inside Job - The Looting of America's Savings & Loans. McGraw—Hill Publishing Co., 1989.

Schor, Juliet B. The Overworked American. Basic Books, 1991.

Stewart, James B. Den of Thieves. Simon & Schuster, 1991.

Tomasko, Robert M. Downsizing: Reshaping the Corporation for the Future. Amacom, 1987.

Walton, Mary. The Deming Management Method. Perigee Books, 1986

About the Author

I have been seated at the table – rather, more accurately, been seated behind the white men seated at the table and told to hold my tongue – at the launch of some of the most radical new business models of the last century. I have had a front row seat for every new finance and economic theory that came down the pike. This is a dubious honor. I have watched these same new business models crash and burn, take jobs, destroy families, make ghost towns of cities, compromise our health and well-being, and rob us of our happiness.

This paper detailed the junk bonds and the savings and loan debacle. There are many more which I will explore in other e-books.

DIANE M. FREANEY

HEART WORK

EMERSON HOUSE ART GALLERY – *Dealer in Cultural Artifacts and Visual Art*
EMERSON HOUSE PRESS – *Publishing Company*
DUNCAN FARMS OREGON – *The future of farming – a 20-acre family farm in Gales Creek, OR*
ROOTED INVESTING – *Bringing capital back to earth*

PROFESSIONAL EXPERIENCE

THEATRES, FOUNDATIONS AND NON-PROFIT ORGANIZATIONS

FREANEY & COMPANY, *Accounting, Audit and Risk Management*	1958-2021
OREGON LIONS SIGHT & HEARING FOUNDATION, *Contract CFO*	2009-2016
FOR THE CHILDREN INC, *Contract CFO*	1998-2015
MUSEUM OF CONTEMPORARY CRAFT, *Interim Director of Finance*	2008-2009
LAKE WORTH PLAYHOUSE, *Executive Director*	2006-2007
CALDWELL THEATRE COMPANY, *Director of Finance*	2005-2006
PLANNED PARENTHOOD, *Chief Financial Officer*	2004-2005
LA JOLLA PLAYHOUSE, *Director of Finance*	2003-2004
FLORIDA ATLANTIC UNIVERSITY FOUNDATION INC. *Chief Financial Officer*	1999-2003
COMMUNITY FOUNDATION OF PALM BEACH & MARTIN COUNTIES, *Interim CFO*	1999
THE PHILADELPHIA FOUNDATION, *Chief Financial and Investment Officer*	1991-1997

CORPORATE

SAFEGUARD BUSINESS SYSTEMS, *Vice President & Treasurer*	1982-1990
CIGNA CORPORATION, *Director Of Business Analysis*	1979-1981
ITT CORPORATION, *Manager Of Financial Control*	1975-1978
KENTON CORPORATION, *Controller*	1973-1975
CITIBANK, *Assistant Vice President*	1971-1972
KPMG, *Audit Staff*	1965-1970

EDUCATION

M.B.A., *Sustainable Systems*, BAINBRIDGE GRADUATE INSTITUTE	2013
Certificate in Food and Agriculture	2013
M.S. *Dynamics of Organizations*, UNIVERSITY OF PENNSYLVANIA	1999
M.B.A., *Marketing*, NEWPORT UNIVERSITY	1982
B.S. *Management & Accounting*, SYRACUSE UNIVERSITY	1965

CONTINUING EDUCATION

HARVARD BUSINESS SCHOOL, *Corporate Financial Management Program*	1980
CORNERSTONE THEATER, *Los Angeles, Residency*	2007
CERTIFICATE IN FUND RAISING, *University of Pennsylvania*	
CERTIFIED PUBLIC ACCOUNTANT, *Florida, New York and Pennsylvania (Retired)*	
CERTIFIED QUICKBOOKS PRO ADVISOR *(Retired)*	

Made in United States
Orlando, FL
11 December 2021

11520573R00046